ALTERNATOR
BOOKS™

# DESIGN
# AND BUILD
# YOUR OWN
# WEBSITE

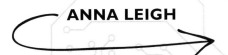 ANNA LEIGH

Lerner Publications ◆ Minneapolis

Lerner Publications Company
A division of Lerner Publishing Group, Inc.
241 First Avenue North
Minneapolis, MN 55401 USA

For reading levels and more information, look up this title at www.lernerbooks.com.

**Library of Congress Cataloging-in-Publication Data**

The Cataloging-in-Publication Data for *Design and Build Your Own Website* is on file at the Library of Congress.
ISBN 978-1-5124-8342-0 (lib. bdg.)
ISBN 978-1-5124-8344-4 (EB pdf)

Manufactured in the United States of America
1-43344-33164-6/20/2017

# CONTENTS

# WEBSITE BUILDING

**DO YOU HAVE AN AMAZING RECIPE FOR CHOCOLATE CAKE THAT THE WORLD JUST *NEEDS* TO KNOW ABOUT?** Do you love learning about Civil War history? Are you working on a really cool art or science project at school? Do you wish you could share your knowledge and skills with the world? Sounds as if you need to build a website.

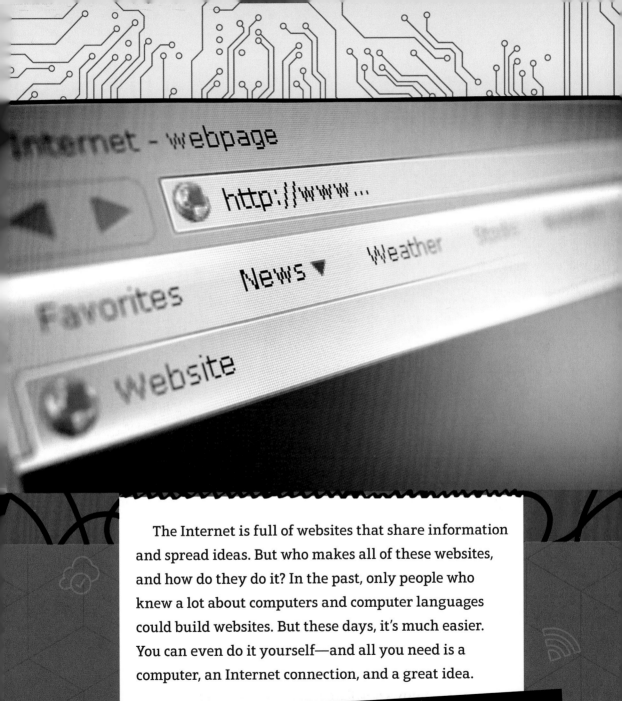

The Internet is full of websites that share information and spread ideas. But who makes all of these websites, and how do they do it? In the past, only people who knew a lot about computers and computer languages could build websites. But these days, it's much easier. You can even do it yourself—and all you need is a computer, an Internet connection, and a great idea.

Ready to build a website? Great—**LET'S GET STARTED!**

# CHAPTER 1

# GETTING STARTED

**STARTING A NEW PROJECT CAN BE INTIMIDATING.** Sometimes it's hard to know where to begin. But the first step is simply to come up with an idea. Projects are always the most fun when you're working with something that excites you, so think about things you enjoy doing and learning about. What websites do you like to visit?

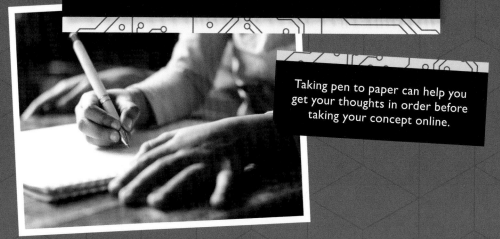

Taking pen to paper can help you get your thoughts in order before taking your concept online.

Tavi Gevinson came to fame building a website called Style Rookie, where she shared her passion for fashion with the world.

Once you have your idea, start planning your site. Think about how the site will look and what information you'll include. Will you have photos on your website? Will everything be on one page, or do you want your website to have separate sections? To help organize your thoughts, draw a map of your website or sketch what you'd like the finished product to look like.

# DECISIONS, DECISIONS

→ **NEXT, YOU'LL THINK ABOUT HOW YOU'RE ACTUALLY GOING TO BUILD THE WEBSITE.** Lots of programs and websites are available to help you. To build your site, you'll need a **domain name**, a **host**, and a website builder. But there are a few things to think about first. Do you want to spend any money on your website? And how much technical knowledge do you have or want to gain?

If you're pinching pennies, never fear! There are plenty of affordable—and even free—ways to build a website.

# CREATIVE TIP

You don't need to know how to code to build a website, but knowing some code can help. Many websites and free online courses are available to teach people about coding. Your school or community might also have a coding class or a club you can join.

For those into the techy side of website building, learning to code can be a lot of fun.

Let's say you want your site to be completely free, and you don't have much technical knowledge. No problem—you can use a free web-building program. These programs will give you a free domain name, free hosting, and even free design **templates** to use for your site. These websites are the easiest kind to build.

Filling in a template with designs that you like is a great way to express your personality.

The library has plenty of print and online resources for you to research website building.

Research the different web hosts, and choose an option that fits your skill level and will work for the kind of website you're planning. And make sure you ask a parent or guardian before you begin working with any programs.

#  IN DEPTH

# HOSTING
# AND DOMAINS

Building a website often costs money. This money pays a company to host the site. It also costs money to buy a personal domain name. When you set up your site through a free hosting site, the host owns your domain name. That's why the name of the site is included in the **URL**. But if you buy your own domain name, the **URL** will look like this: mydomainname.com.

Fashion guru Chelsea Lankford learned the ins and outs of building websites to create her own site all about style. Here she poses for a photo taken for her site.

The URL for your cool new instructional baking site might look like this: http://www.muffinsandmore.webhost.com.

When you've found a host that you like, you'll create an account. The program will probably ask for your name and e-mail address. Then you'll choose the domain name of your website. Because you are using a free host, the domain name will also include the name of the hosting site, and the URL will look like this: mydomainname.webhost.com. Choose a domain name that is simple and easy to remember. The web host will tell you whether the name you choose is available. You might have to try several different names before you find one that is available. Once your account is set up, it's time for the fun part—building your site.

## CHAPTER 2

# HONING YOUR SITE

**IT'S TIME TO PUT YOUR DESIGN PLAN INTO ACTION.** Your web builder will probably have several templates for you to choose from. These layouts will show you where to put photos and text. They will have a color **palette** and **fonts** in place. You'll probably have the option to make changes to these templates, colors, and fonts to make your site match your plan.

Picking out favorite fonts and colors is a task that many website builders enjoy.

# IN DEPTH
## HTML AND CSS

Maybe you're ready for more of a challenge, and you want to try designing your site using **HTML** and **CSS**. These are languages that **web browsers** can understand. When you use HTML and CSS to write instructions, your browser can follow your ideas to make things look the way you want them to. This method is a little more complicated, but it gives you more control over the design of your site—and you'll have a very special and useful skill!

Summer and after-school classes might teach HTML and CSS.

Think about your website as you look through the templates. If you plan to include a large number of images, you'll want the template to have big spaces for images. Maybe you want to include a blog on your website—many templates will include that option. Some templates are very simple, and others have spaces to include lots of different bits of text and photos.

If showing how to build or make things step-by-step is important on your site, you'll probably want a template that includes ample space for photos.

Into photography? That can be a handy passion when it comes to website building. Great photos can really enhance a site.

Once you have decided on a template, you'll begin changing it and adding your own content to the site. Your website builder will probably make it pretty easy for you to move sections around and create new pages and tabs. Then you can begin to upload your photos and add your text.

# TEST IT OUT

**AFTER YOU'VE DESIGNED AND PLACED ALL THE CONTENT ON YOUR WEBSITE, YOU SHOULD TEST THE SITE.** Your website builder will probably have a function that allows you to preview your site in a web browser. Test your website on several different browsers and on a mobile device to see how everything looks.

Some features might show up differently on a smaller screen or in a different browser. You may want to tweak some parts of your website to make sure they look good in each place. You might also ask a friend or family member to take a look at your website so you can get feedback about whether your website is easy to read and use. Once your site has all its content and images and it looks exactly the way you want it to, it's time to publish the site!

See what your site looks like on a phone as well as on a desktop computer.

# CREATIVE TIP

To make sure your site looks great and is easy to read, choose simple fonts and colors that look good together. Some colors should be dark, and some should be brighter—but you shouldn't use more than five colors. Otherwise, the site might look too busy.

Colors bring style to a website. Just be sure not to go overboard with color!

# CHAPTER 3

# SHARING YOUR WORK

**HIT THE PUBLISH BUTTON.** Your website is on the Internet! If you type your URL into a web browser, your very own site will appear—but how will other people find your website?

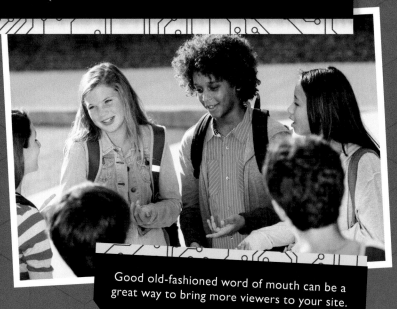

Good old-fashioned word of mouth can be a great way to bring more viewers to your site.

# ANDREW SUTHERLAND

When Andrew Sutherland was a junior in high school, he published a website that would help him learn vocabulary words for his French class. He called the site Quizlet. Andrew told his friends about the site, and they liked it too. Eventually, Andrew realized that other students might find the site useful, so he made sure anyone could create a profile. Ten years later, Quizlet is used by millions of students around the world.

First, you should decide who you want to see your website. As with any activity online, it is important to keep your website safe. You might choose to protect your site with a password so that whoever visits the site must enter the password to see any content. This is an especially good idea if you have shared any photos or if this is a school project and information such as the name of your school is visible on the site.

# BUILDING AN AUDIENCE

→ **IF YOU WANT TO SHARE YOUR SITE WITH A LARGER AUDIENCE, FIRST CHECK WITH A PARENT OR GUARDIAN TO MAKE SURE IT'S OK.** Then you can start sharing your site. One of the easiest ways to share your site is to post the URL on social media. This way all of your contacts will see the link.

Check in with a trusted adult before sharing anything online.

Updating your site each day with a new photo of an amazing nature scene or a selfie of you in a fun new location can draw repeat visitors.

Think about how you can encourage visitors to return to your site. If it looks the same every time people visit it, they might lose interest. But if you update your site often, people will keep coming to see what's new. Maybe you'll upload a new photo every weekend. You can also repost the URL to your site on social media each time you update the site—maybe someone new will see the link!

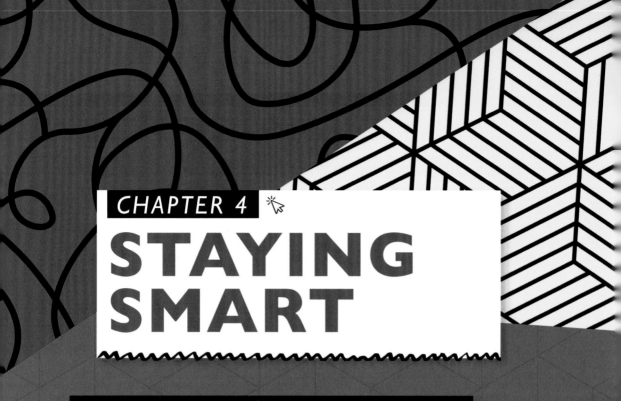

# CHAPTER 4

# STAYING SMART

**CREATING A WEBSITE IS A LOT OF FUN.** And it's even more fun when you know that people are looking at your site, learning from the information you've posted, and enjoying your photos. How do you show your audience that you appreciate their loyalty?

It can be exciting to check your site and see appreciative comments from readers.

Feedback from others—both friends and strangers, online and off—can be the most valuable tool you have for improving your site.

Chances are that when you posted the link to your social media profiles, people gave you feedback. Maybe they made comments or shared your post. You may have also included a section on your site for people to leave comments. These comments are an important part of what is known as an online community.

# CREATIVE TIP

Pay attention to the posts that get your site lots of viewers. Continue to use the methods that seem most popular. If you include photos with the link, the post will look more intriguing on social media. You might also include a clever title or a fun description for your post. This will catch people's interest, and they'll want to see more.

Through comments and feedback, you can learn what people like about your website and what they would like to see more of. You don't need to make every change that is suggested in the comments. But you can respond to comments and thank people for their feedback. You might also visit other websites and leave responses for their creators. Feedback helps people become better at creating, designing, and sharing content that others are interested in. And because you know the basics of website building and design, you can continue to improve your skills too!

# JULIETTE BRINDAK

When Juliette Brindak was thirteen, she came up with an idea for a website aimed at young girls. Juliette's parents helped her design and build a social media site called Miss O and Friends. The popular site included advice, quizzes, and games for girls. Juliette continued working on the site even after graduating from college. She loved creating a space for girls that would help them build confidence and self-esteem.

# WEBSITE CHECKLIST

**ARE YOU EXCITED ABOUT CREATING YOUR WEBSITE?** You have all the skills you need. It's time to use them. Here are all the steps to create your very own online space. Have fun!

1. Come up with an idea for your website. Think about the things you love to do and learn about and the kinds of websites you enjoy visiting.

2. Plan your site. Decide what sections, information, and images to include. Draw a map of your site and its design.

3. Research website builders and hosts. Choose one that matches your skill level and will work to create the site you have in mind. Make sure you check whether the host is free!

4. Sign up for an account with the program you have chosen.

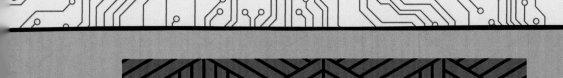

5. Choose a domain name for your site. Pick something simple and easy for people to remember.

6. Choose a design template for your site. Think about all the sections, content, and images you plan to include, and think about whether your template will work with your design.

7. Create your site. Upload your content, and make changes to the template, colors, and fonts.

8. Test your site. Make sure it looks right on several different browsers and screens. Ask someone to review your site and give you feedback.

9. Publish your website!

10. Think about how public you want your site and its content to be. Consider adding a password to your site if you only want to share it with friends and family.

11. Share your site by telling people about it and sharing links to the site on social media.

12. Update your website with new content to build your audience.

13. Participate in your online community by responding to feedback and giving other website designers feedback.

14. Keep practicing your skills to get even better at designing and building websites.

# GLOSSARY

**CSS:** a language used to communicate design elements for files on the Internet. *CSS* stands for *cascading style sheets*.

**domain name:** the main part of a website address

**fonts:** styles for letters and numbers

**host:** a computer that controls communications in a network or that administers a database

**HTML:** a language used to mark up documents so that Internet browsers understand what to display. *HTML* stands for *hypertext markup language*.

**palette:** the set of colors used in a design or artwork

**templates:** patterns or basic formats used as guides to create something

**URL:** the address of a resource on the Internet. *URL* stands for *uniform resource locator*.

**web browsers:** computer programs used for accessing websites on the Internet

# FURTHER INFORMATION

BBC: What Makes a Good Web Page?
http://www.bbc.co.uk/guides/zgx3b9q#zctgr82

Hatter, Clyde. *Build your Own Website: Create with Code.* New York: Scholastic, 2016.

Kenney, Karen Latchana. *Create Your Own Blog.* Minneapolis: Lerner Publications, 2018.

KidsHealth: Your Online Identity
http://kidshealth.org/en/kids/online-id.html?WT.ac=p-ra#

Lindeen, Mary. *Smart Online Communication: Protecting your Digital Footprint.* Minneapolis: Lerner Publications, 2016.

Lissa Explains It All: Web Page Basics
http://www.lissaexplains.com/basics.shtml

McManus, Sean. *How to Code in 10 Easy Lessons: Learn How to Design and Code Your Very Own Computer Game.* Lake Forest, CA: Walter Foster Jr., 2015.

Wainewright, Max. *How to Code: A Step-by-Step Guide to Computer Coding.* New York: Sterling Children's Books, 2016.

Web Design for Kids
https://webdesign.tutsplus.com/series/web-design-for-kids--cms-823

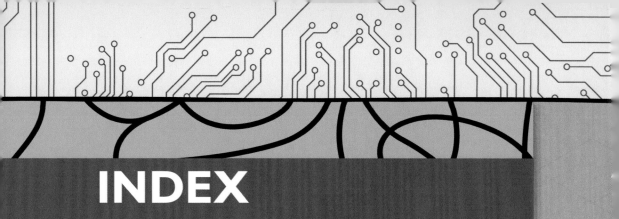

# INDEX

# PHOTO ACKNOWLEDGMENTS

The images in this book are used with the permission of: DESIGN ELEMENTS: Iliveinoctober/Shutterstock.com; iStock.com/fonikum; iStock.com/Sylverarts; iStock.com/chaluk; iStock.com/pixaroma; iStock.com/chekat; iStock.com/ulimi; iStock.com/slalomp; CONTENT: iStock.com/MalyDesigner, p. 4; iStock.com/Henrik5000, p. 5; iStock.com/Liderina, p. 6; EXImages/Alamy Stock Photo, p. 7; iStock.com/AnthiaCumming, p. 8; iStock.com/Belyaevskiy, p. 9; Oniks Astarit/Shutterstock.com, p. 10; Sebestyen Balint/Shutterstock.com, p. 10; iStock.com/GlobalStock, p. 11; Tribune Content Agency LLC/Alamy Stock Photo, p. 12; Arina P Habich/Shutterstock.com, p. 13; cosmaa/Shutterstock.com, p. 14; iStock.com/KatarzynaBialasiewicz, p. 15; iStock.com/Weekend Images Inc., p. 16; iStock.com/studiocasper, p. 17; Anna Hoychuk/Shutterstock.com, p. 18; Bokeh Art Photo/Shutterstock.com, p. 19; iStock.com/kali9, p. 20; iStock.com/monkeybusinessimages, p. 22; iStock.com/MattRied, p. 23; iStock.com/fstop123, p. 24; iStock.com/gawrav, p. 25; © Jakub Mosur/flickr.com (CC BY-NC 2.0), p. 27.

Front cover: © Hero Images/Getty Images.